Magnificent Mind Masters Multiplication

Ellen Arnold

Illustrations by Deborah Farber

Zephyr Press®

Reaching Their Highest Potential

Tucson, Arizona

Acknowledgments

—To Russ, whose number-smart part developed at an awesome speed—

Creating books takes work, but when you have a great team, the process can be joyful. Deborah Farber's picture-smart part helped develop my ideas into a wonderful visual presence. Marti Arnold's word- and number-smart parts were an invaluable asset in helping me be clear, concise, and consistent. Without their patience, ideas, and support, this project would still be in my mind rather than in your hands.

Magnificent Mind Masters Multiplication

Grades K–4

Printed in the United States of America

ISBN 1-56976-116-7

Editor: Bonnie Lewis
Design & Production: Daniel Miedaner
Cover Design: Daniel Miedaner
Illustrations: Deborah Farber

Published by
Zephyr Press
P.O. Box 66006
Tucson, Arizona 87528-6006
http://zephyrpress.com
http://giftsforteachers.com

Library of Congress Cataloging-in-Publication Data

Arnold, Ellen, 1944-
Magnificent Mind masters multiplication / by Ellen Arnold ; illustrated by Deborah Farber.
p. cm.
ISBN 1-56976-116-7
1. Multiplication—Juvenile literature. [1. Multiplication.] I. Farber, Deborah, ill. II. Title.

QA115 .A76 2000
513.2'13—dc21 00-036845

Magnificent Mind Masters Multiplication

A Note to Teachers and Parents:

Teachers expect students to store multiplication facts in their automatic memories, but many students do not know how to do this. Magnificent Mind models strategies that students can use when they mindfully memorize information. Join her to learn strategies for memorizing the sevens. **MI Strategies for Kids**, *a teacher/parent manual, describes a lesson plan that will help make this book a most useful tool for your students.*

Teacher: *Magnificent Mind, have you learned your sevens?*

MM: Huh? Yes, ah, I think so.

Teacher: *Are you sure?*

MM: Well, no, not really. I have tried to learn them. Honest, I have. I studied and studied.

Teacher: *Magnificent, I know you want to do well in school, but you have got to learn to take control of your mind. Now, please get these facts to stick.*

MM: OK. I'll really try.

Teacher: *Now class, tomorrow we will be having a test on the sevens. I want everyone to get 100.*

MM: How am I going to get these numbers to stick? They are so hard to remember. I get them all mixed up. I do try to remember, but the numbers all run together. I think I have them and then someone quizzes me and my mind is a blank. I'd better check my strategy bank to see if there are some strategies I can use.

As soon as Magnificent got home, she checked her strategy bank. She found strategies for reading, strategies for listening, strategies for skiing, and strategies for spelling, but she could not find any strategies for remembering math facts. She decided to ask her friends, the Smart Parts. She especially wanted to talk with Number Smart. She figured that Number Smart would know a number of strategies to learn math. And maybe her other smart parts could help her like they had before. Magnificent put on her strategy bank backpack and set off to find her Smart Parts on Intelligence Avenue.

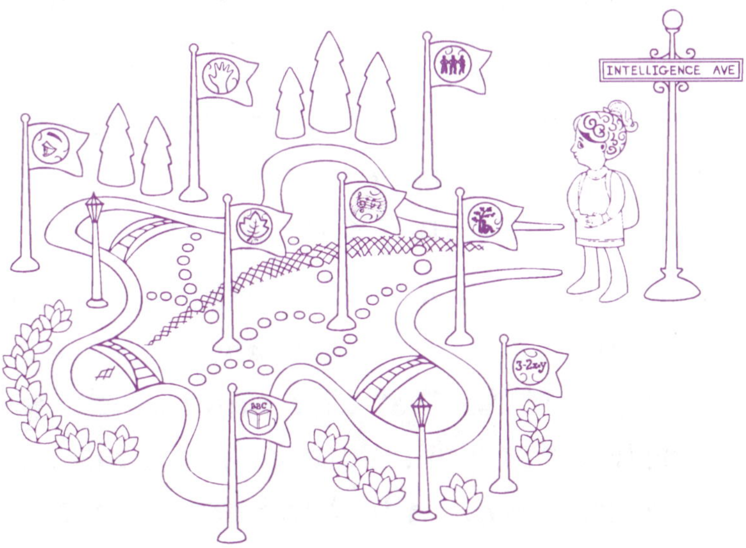

NS: If I had three dogs and my friend gave me four birds, then one flew away, and then I found six kittens in the back yard, and the one dog died, then I bought three fish and then I gave two kittens to friends, how many kittens would I have?

MM: Number Smart, what are you doing?

NS: Using my numbers. I like making up problems and solving them. Can you tell me the answer?

MM: Can you repeat the problem?

NS: Sure. If I had three dogs, and my friend gave me four birds, then one flew away, and then I found six kittens in the back yard, and one dog died, then I bought three fish and then I gave two kittens to friends, how many kittens would I have?

MM: Well, I think you said you found six kittens and gave two away. So that would leave four.

NS: Excellent, Magnificent. You really listened well. And I can tell you have been practicing your problem solving. What can I do for you?

MM: Do you have a formula or pattern to help with memorizing math facts? I'm having a terrible time. They just don't stick. I can do adding and subtracting but multiplication facts are so hard. And we are having a test tomorrow, and I just

don't know what to do. I couldn't find any strategies in my strategy bank that seemed to help. And since you are so good at numbers, I figured I should come to you first.

NS: Very logical, Magnificent. I have lots of strategies I use for multiplication. But I never had to work at it very hard, because learning numbers was easy for me. I had trouble with some other parts of school, especially creative writing, but numbers, well, they just don't add up. Do you have specific math facts that you want to learn?

MM: Let's do the sevens. They seem to be the hardest for me and we are supposed to know them by tomorrow.

NS: OK. What I do is pay attention to patterns. Start with ones that are easy.

MM: But I don't think I know any of them.

NS: I doubt that. I think you know more than you think you do. Let's analyze 7 x 10. Count by tens: 10, 20, 30, 40, 50, 60, 70. Is there any pattern?

MM: Well, they all end in 0.

NS: Always, precisely. Anything else?

MM: Well, 10 is 1 x 10 and 20 is 2 x 10. So I guess the 70 is 7 x 10.

What is a pattern you have used in math?

NS: Exactly.

MM: So each one has its own number first and then is followed by a zero?

NS: That is the pattern. And once you understand the pattern, you don't have to memorize these at all.

MM: But my teacher wants me to know them really fast. Not just figure them out.

NS: Then rehearse the pattern. Let's try a harder one, because it sounds like you already know the tens. And if you know one set of patterns, it helps you learn others.

MM: Okay, then let's try the nines. They seem hard.

NS: That's a good choice because you can use the pattern for tens to figure out and learn the nines. 7 x 9 is 63. The formula I use is to count by tens and subtract the number of tens you had. For example, what is 10 x 4?

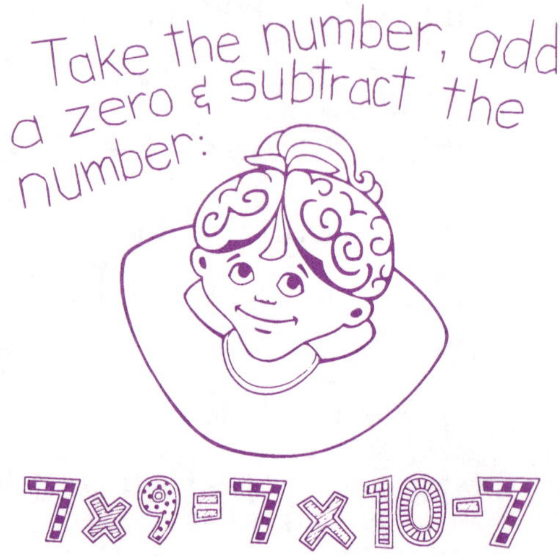

MM: A four and a zero, 40.

NS: Now subtract the 4 and what do you get?

MM: 36.

NS: Great. Do you understand the process?

MM: I think so. 9 is one less than 10, and so you take one away from each of the four 10s. So 4 from 40 is 36?

NS: Exactly.

MM: Will this work for all the nines?

NS: Always.

MM: So that means, if I want 7 x 9, I do 70 (because that is 10 x 7) and then I subtract the 7?

NS: Yep.

MM: And that is 63. That is easy!

NS: You can use the "Find the Pattern" strategy to quickly figure out the nines if you forget. Right now it may take you a long time to do, but if you practice this strategy many times, you will get faster and faster at it.

MM: Thanks, Number Smart. I'll look for the pattern. But I wonder if there are other ways to learn these facts.

NS: Well, why don't you plan a research expedition around Intelligence Avenue and collect some more strategies for math facts? I'm sure the other Smart Parts will have ideas for you.

So Magnificent paced Intelligence Avenue, which is where all the Smart Parts lived. Each one had a special location on this windy, wiggly path. Soon, Magnificent discovered Self Smart looking up at the sky.

MM: Self Smart, what are you doing?

SS: Thinking about the universe and what it is like.

MM: What do you mean?

SS: Well, you know how important it is to love yourself, to honor yourself, and to accept yourself?

MM: Yes.

SS: And that you are totally unique?

MM: Yes.

SS: And sometimes, on earth, we forget all those things. The universe is where we find out the real truth to life.

MM: Well, do you think you can help me find out the real truth about memorizing multiplication? I am having trouble with math facts, like the sevens. I don't know them. They just don't stick.

SS: You are one person, right?

MM: Yes.

SS: In the universe, you are accepted for yourself. Well, that is just like the ones. No matter what number you are, if you multiply it by one, you are still the same number. One is like the universe—it just accepts you for what you are.

MM: So 1 x 7 is still 7?

SS: Yes, and 1 x 4 is still 4 and 1 x 87 is still 87.

MM: Hey. That is cool. I think I understand the ones now.

SS: Good. But it sounds like you think you don't know any of the times tables. I can't let you believe that.

MM: Why not? I don't know them.

SS: I think you know more than you think you do, Magnificent. Your mind is such a wonderful thing. It is so much easier to learn something when you believe you already know a little bit about it, then you only have to work at the portion that you might not know.

MM: Hmm. I don't know. I guess I know the ones.

SS: How come you remember the ones?

MM: I don't know. Maybe they just make sense.

SS: So if the rest of the number facts make sense, then will you be able to remember them?

MM: Maybe, but I can't seem to make numbers make sense. They are just numbers.

SS: Here are the seven facts or multiples. Do any of these numbers have any special meaning for you?

Which of these numbers can you connect to best and why?

MM: Hmm. I guess 56. It is where Brilliant Brain and I live. Our address is 56 Intelligence Avenue.

SS: Good. Now think of a way to remember 8 x 7 = 56.

MM: This is hard, but I can think of one thing. All of the 8 Smart Parts live in my neighborhood, and they are there every day of the week.

SS: **So 8 Smart Parts x 7 days = 56. 8 x 7 = 56.**

MM: Yes, that's right.

SS: Do you think these numbers will stick now?

MM: Yes, I do! This was great. What do you call this strategy, Self Smart?

SS: I would call it the "Connect to Yourself" strategy. You can use it with any numbers.

MM: Thanks, I will put this in my backpack and definitely try it.

Magnificent thoughtfully strolled across a bridge. Through the trees she heard someone say:

PS: Magnificent, you look very serious today.

MM: Oh, hi, People Smart.

PS: What is the problem?

MM: Today's problem is the number 7. I need to know the multiplication facts, and they don't always stay in my head. I need to know them for tomorrow, and I guess I need some more strategies. Do you know any strategies that will help me?

PS: Numbers can be hard to remember. And multiplication takes lots of strategies. Do you know the Rule of Zero?

MM: No.

PS: Well, no matter what you multiply times zero, it is still zero. If we ate all of our snack and didn't have any left, we would have nothing. But if we double what we had, what would we have?

MM: Nothing, if you double nothing, you still have nothing.

PS: Right.

MM: I think I understand. But if you have nothing, you can't write it down, can you? I mean, it is nothing.

PS: Ah, great thinking, Maggie. We have a special shape we use to represent nothing. It is an empty circle.

MM: You mean a zero?

PS: Exactly. A zero or an O or an empty ring.

MM: Like a friendship ring?

PS: If you have a ring that you haven't given to anyone, then it doesn't have anyone in it.

MM: So a zero is something with nothing inside.

PS: Right. Now you understand what a zero is. But when we are trying to remember numbers, we connect each one to a person. We know lots of people, and so we never run out of connections.

MM: How does that strategy work?

PS: Well, let's take the number O. Do you know about Dr. Martin Luther King? He believed in zero fighting.

MM: What does that mean?

PS: He wanted people to change by using their words and their problem-solving skills, but not fighting or violence. So he is a good symbol for the rule of zero. No matter who he was with or how angry he got, he would never fight. Zero fighting!

MM: Even if a bad guy tried to hurt him, he wouldn't fight?

PS: That's right. He would sit quietly and refuse to cooperate with things he thought were wrong. He would talk and he would listen, but he would not fight.

MM: How can that help me with my sevens?

PS: Let's see if we can find the pattern with numbers:

$$0 \times 1 = 0$$
$$0 \times 2 = 0$$
$$0 \times 3 = 0$$
$$0 \times 25 = ?$$

MM: 0 again?

PS: Yes. Anything multiplied by nothing is still empty.

MM: Cool. I think I got it.

PS: So what is 0 x 7?

MM: 0?

PS: Yes. And what if I turn it around and say 7 x 0?

MM: Well, that didn't change anything. It is still 0.

PS: So now you know the rule of zero.

MM: That's great. I understand and I didn't have to memorize anything. You make it so easy. Thanks, People Smart, for the "Rule of Zero" strategy. I am feeling much better because I like imagining different people for different numbers. Right now, I am going to continue around Intelligence Avenue and see if the other Smart Parts have any more strategies for learning the sevens. Want to come?

PS: Sorry, Maggie, we have work to do, but we are sure you will get some other great ideas from the other Smart Parts.

Magnificent drew near the brightly colored stone path that led to one of the bridges across Intelligence Avenue. There, she saw Picture Smart painting.

MM: Picture Smart, what are you painting?

PS: Hi, Maggie. It's a picture of our neighborhood here on Intelligence Avenue.

MM: That looks great. But I could use your point of view. I know how good you are at pictures. Are there any pictures that will help me learn the multiplication facts? I am having trouble memorizing them. Especially the sevens.

PS: Sevens, huh? Let's focus on a specific one. Which one do you want to store?

MM: How about 7 x 4? That one is hard.

PS: Oh, here's an image. Look here. Do you know what this is?

1	2	3	4	5	6	7
8	9	10	11	12	13	14
15	16	17	18	19	20	21
22	23	24	25	26	27	28

MM: It looks like a calendar. Is it the one for the month of February?

PS: Yes. Can you see the number of days in the week?

MM: 7.

PS: And how many weeks?

MM: 4.

PS: Now count the days.

Which month is your birthday in? What does that grid look like?

MM: . . . 24, 25, 26, 27, 28. There are 28.

PS: Right. So we have 7 days and 4 weeks, and that's 28.

MM: Great. Are all months 28 days?

PS: All months have at least 28 days. But only February stops at 28, except during a leap year, when it has 29.

MM: So now when I think of 7 x 4, I can think of February?

PS: Sure. What picture do you associate with February?

MM: Valentine's Day. That is one of my favorite holidays.

PS: So let's draw hearts around your 7 x 4, and now you have 28.

MM: I got it. I can see it. Thanks, Picture Smart. I'll put the "Draw a Grid" strategy in my strategy bank.

Maggie continued her journey over the hill and through the park on Intelligence Avenue until she saw Nature Smart up in a tree.

MM: Nature Smart, what are you doing?

NS: I am looking at the interesting shapes of the leaves on this silver maple tree. What are you doing, Magnificent?

MM: I am trying to locate some new strategies. I have to learn the sevens and I am not good at memorizing number facts. Do you have a strategy for me?

NS: Well, climb up here and let's observe the woods for a while, and maybe we can come up with something. The trees often give me answers to questions I have.

MM: I never thought of trees being smart. But how am I going to learn the sevens? Like how much is 7 x 5?

NS: Look carefully at a leaf in this tree. What do you notice?

MM: Well, it is green and has little tubes in it.

NS: Anything else about the shape of the leaf?

MM: It is kind of like a hand—it has five things; they look something like fingers.

NS: Good. Now look at this smaller leaf. Is it the same?

MM: Yes, it still has five fingers, but they are smaller.

I'd guess this is a baby leaf, but even though it has been alive less time, it still has five fingers.

NS: So each leaf on a silver maple has five fingers. We call them lobes. Do all trees have leaves with five lobes?

MM: All the ones I see on this tree, but the elm tree in my front yard doesn't look like this at all. It doesn't have fingers, just ridges like a saw. And the pine tree over there doesn't have leaves. It has sharp needles.

NS: Excellent analysis, Maggie. You really have been paying attention to nature.

MM: But how will that help me learn the sevens?

NS: Well, let's see. Look at the shape of this branch. What does it look like to you?

MM: It kind of looks like a 7.

NS: Aha! So a 7 for the branch and 5 lobes for each leaf. If we multiply 7 x 5 we get 35. And a silver maple grows to 35 meters high.

Look out your window and see if you can find something that reminds you of a 7.

MM: Hmm. 35 huh? A branch of 7 and lobes of 5 and a height of 35.

NS: That's right, Magnificent. Is that a link you can remember?

MM: Yes. Thanks for the strategy, Nature Smart. What do you call this?

NS: How about the "Observe Carefully" strategy?

MM: This is a good addition to my strategy bank. Thanks, Nature Smart.

Magnificent marched down Intelligence Avenue, her head high, loudly stomping on the stones. She was reviewing what she had learned so far and feeling better about the sevens. But she still had some to learn. Then she heard a sound, like someone jumping.

MM: Body Smart, what are you doing?

BS: I am learning to hop like a kangaroo.

MM: Why?

BS: Just for fun. I always thought I would like to be a kangaroo. Then I could bounce all over and no one would get upset with me. What are you doing, Maggie?

MM: Trying to build up my supply of strategies. My strategy bank is getting fuller, but I still have some things to learn. I need some more strategies to learn math facts. Do you have any ideas?

BS: We could bounce them.

MM: What do you mean?

BS: When I want to memorize something, I just attach it to a movement and keep doing the movement. Come bounce with me. Jump over to my starting line over here. I have it marked with two shoe prints, so I know exactly where to start.

MM: 1, 2, 3, 4, 5, 6, 7...

BS: Good. Now let's do 7 back the other way and we will be back where we started.

MM: 8, 9, 10, 11, 12, 13, 14.

BS: See, if you bounce 7 times and do 2 sets you have 14 bounces.

MM: Body Smart—wait, give me a chance to breathe! I guess I am not in as good shape as you—14 bounces is a lot. But that was fun. So let me make sure I have this right. I stand on the footprints. I bounce seven times. Then I turn around and bounce back to the shoeprint, counting as I go.

BS: Yes. That is right. Now try it again.

MM: 1.....7, 8....14

BS: Now keep repeating the formula as you move. 7 x 2 is 14. 7 x 2 = 14. 7 x 2 = 14.

MM: Start with a shoe and act like a kangaroo, then you have 14 = 7 x 2.

BS: What do you think of my bouncing strategy?

MM: Well, I can see how it will work for homework, but I don't think I can use it in school. My teachers might not like it if I bounced around in class.

BS: When I am in school or somewhere where I am not supposed to move, I just think of the bouncing or the moving in my head. As long as I have practiced it outside of school, I am able to remember it when I get to school. And then I remember it real well. I can squeeze my legs like I am bouncing, but not really move. Without movement, it is really hard for me to learn anything new. But I love to pretend I am a kangaroo. Do you have another one you want to learn?

MM: Well, 7 x 7 is hard, too. But I don't think I can bounce that many times.

BS: Hmm. Let me think. Do you know anything about football?

MM: A little.

BS: Well, when you score a touchdown and you get the extra point, you get 7 points.

MM: Yes, 6 for the touchdown and 1 for the kick afterwards.

BS: And 7 x 7 means you have a lot of points, right? One of my favorite teams is the 49ers. And 7 x 7 = 49.

MM: That is a great way to remember this math fact. I can add the "Connect to a Sport" strategy to my strategy bank.

Magnificent had collected some cool strategies, and her backpack was getting heavy. But she still had some sevens she didn't know. As she continued to stride down the trail of Intelligence Avenue, she heard Word Smart reciting.

MM: Word Smart, what do you say?

WS: Hi, Magnificent. If I read you correctly, you are a bit bothered today.

MM: You are right. I am trying to learn my math facts. I have a test of the sevens tomorrow, and I am collecting strategies. Do you have any to add to my strategy bank?

WS: Let me check in my dictionary. ***Math facts: specific calculations that need to be overlearned so they become automatic.*** Is that right?

MM: I guess so, but I can't get them to stick. I mean, some are okay, but some are really hard, like 7 x 3 and 7 x 6. Do you have some clues?

WS: I like to use letters to help me remember. Today, I am really paying attention to the letter ***e.*** There are so many words with ***e*** and it often makes different sounds. But maybe I can use an ***e*** to help you. 7 x 3 = 21.

- ➤ *Seven* has two *e*s.
- ➤ *Three* has two *e*s.
- ➤ *Twenty-one* has two *e*s.
- ➤ I love *e*s.

See the many ways *e*s appear in words?

MM: I guess I do. What you just did makes sense, but I am not sure I will remember it.

WS: How about building an acrostic?

MM: A what?

WS: I'll show you.

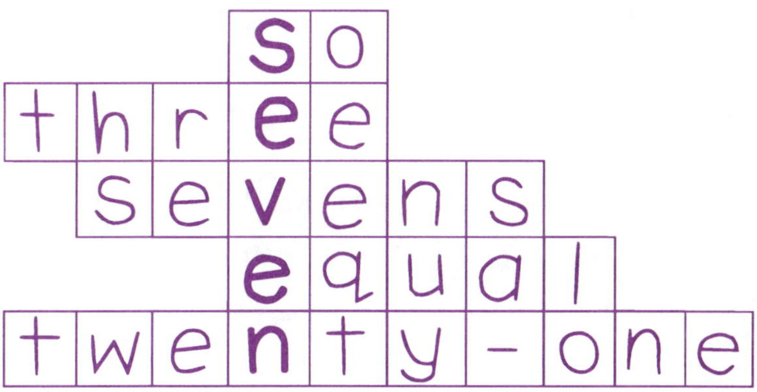

MM: That is kind of cool. I never saw anyone write words that way before.

WS: It is a fun way to do it. I like playing with word associations. I also like to write poetry.

MM: How can poetry help me learn math facts?

WS: Poetry is just a different way of saying things, but poetry makes you think differently because you really have to play with the words and what they mean.

MM: I don't think I have ever written a poem.

WS: Well, let's write a poem together. We could do a haiku. It is a special kind of poem where you have to pick your words carefully, but once you put all the words together, you get something really neat.

MM: How do you do it?

WS: Well, which fact of the sevens do you want to learn? We need to start with some words.

MM: How about 7 x 6. That is a hard one.

WS: OK. I know that 7 x 6 = 42. Now I have to think of something that has meaning with the number 42. Hmm. I know. Have you ever seen a NASCAR race?

MM: No. Isn't that with racecars?

WS: Yes. And they can have 42 cars at the beginning of the race. And at our local track, they use Unocal 76 gas. So 7 x 6 = 42. Now let's write a poem about it:

42 NASCARS
Running out of energy
76 gas

MM: Wow! You got all that into just a few words.

WS: And these words can help you remember numbers.

MM: I like that strategy. I'll have to practice it, though!

MM: Thanks, Word Smart. You have helped me with the sevens I didn't know. I think I need to review them all now.

Magnificent meandered across the bridge and back toward home. But she stopped when she heard some music.

MM: Music Smart, are you free?
My math task is bothering me.
I need to know my math facts fast.
I need to learn them so they last.

MS: This can be easy, you will see.
Don't let numbers make you angry.
Together we will sing anew
All your problems in review.

MM: I need to learn the sevens table
To show the teacher I am able.
I get numbers so confused
Choices, choices. Which to use?
I need to make the numbers stick
But from my mind they fall out quick.
I've gathered seven strategies.
Can you help me review them please?

MS: Sevens are fun when you give them a beat
Make them automatic, say them, repeat!
Put them in order and go to the start
Put them in a sevens chart.

Martin Luther King would never fight,
A hero of **zero,** making things right.
With 7, the universe plays no game
7 x 1 is **7** just the same.

7 x 2 begins on a shoe
Count **14** bounces like a kangaroo.
3 x 7 equals **21**
Seven hides inside for some anagram fun.

February has a great claim to fame,
28 days in a calendar frame.
A maple tree shows us 7 x 5
As it grows to be **35** meters high.

7 x 6 cars will keep the pace.
42 cars hope to win the race.
7 x 7 equals **49,**
Score seven touchdowns and win every time.

7 x 8 is a place that I go,
Number **56** is the home that I know.
7 x 9 is a big **63.**
When you know the tens it is really easy.
7 x 10 is **70,** oh!
These are the sevens, from ten down to zero.

Now see how easy the sevens can be
When you use the right strategy?
The rhymes, the pictures, the patterns are fun.
Find the connections and soon you'll be done!

MM: Music Smart, you sure can rhyme
And that helps make the sevens mine.
These strategies make me realize
That even I can memorize.
I owe you so much, you have my thanks
For giving me songs for my strategy banks.

Magnificent Mind managed to master multiplication. She used all her smart parts to help her come up with strategies she could use. And so if you get stuck trying to learn a new math fact, think about the strategies you can use. And when you do, you will be maximizing your mind, just like Magnificent.